HISTORY'S VILLAINS

JOSEPH STALIN

Scott Ingram

BLACKBIRCH®
PRESS

THOMSON
GALE

San Diego • Detroit • New York • San Francisco • Cleveland
New Haven, Conn. • Waterville, Maine • London • Munich

THOMSON

★

™

GALE

© 2002 by Blackbirch Press™. Blackbirch Press™ is an imprint of The Gale Group, Inc., a division of Thomson Learning, Inc.

Blackbirch Press™ and Thomson Learning™ are trademarks used herein under license.

For more information, contact
The Gale Group, Inc.
27500 Drake Rd.
Farmington Hills, MI 48331-3535
Or you can visit our Internet site at http://www.gale.com

Photo Credits: Cover, pages 6, 25, 32, 38, 42, 47, 56, 66, 68, 80, 83, 86, 89, 95, 97,101 © historypictures.com; page 9, 12, 30, 52, 55, 76 © CORBIS; pages 15, 16, 46, 71, 74 © Hulton-Deutsch Collection/CORBIS; pages 18, 44, 57 © Bettmann/CORBIS Collection; page 34 © Archivo Iconografico, S.A./CORBIS; page 40 © Austrian Archives/CORBIS

LIBRARY OF CONGRESS CATALOGING-IN-PUBLICATION DATA

Ingram, Scott
  Joseph Stalin / by Scott Ingram
    p. cm. — (History's greatest villains)
  Summary: Chronicles the youth, rise to power, and dictatorial reign of the Soviet Union's Joseph Stalin.
  Includes bibliographical references and index.
   ISBN 1-56711-626-4 (hardback : alk. paper)
   1. Stalin, Joseph, 1879-1953—Juvenile literature. 2. Heads of state—Soviet Union—Biography—Juvenile literature. 3. Soviet Union—History—1925-1953—Juvenile literature. [1. Stalin, Joseph 1879-1953. 2. Heads of state. 3. Soviet Union—History—1925-1953.] I. Title. II. Series.
   DK268.S8 K37 2003
   947.084'2'092—dc21   2002008427

Printed in United States
10 9 8 7 6 5 4 3 2 1

CONTENTS

Introduction: "The Devil's Hoof"

In the late 1800s, young boys in Gori, a town in the Russian province of Georgia, played a game called *krivi*. The game was a series of boxing and wrestling matches between one team made up of wealthy boys and one of boys from poor families. The wealthier boys, who were better-fed and stronger, usually won the *krivi* contests. The cleverest fighter on either team, however, was the smallest member of the poor team. His name was Soso Dzhugashvili.

Teammates and opponents were amazed that Soso was able to absorb vicious beatings from bigger, stronger boys without even a whimper. They admired his trickiness when he pretended to give up in a fight, then attacked his opponent from behind the moment the opponent turned his back.

Although he was small for his age, Soso's toughness enabled him to form friendships with older boys. The biggest and best fighter among the wealthy boys in Gori, Mikhail Peradze, tried to get Soso to join his team. Soso refused because he wanted to be the top fighter on his own team rather than just a good fighter on the other team. Nevertheless, the two boys became good friends, and Peradze actually looked up to Soso.

On a warm day in the late 1880s, Soso, Peradze, and a group of other boys decided to swim in the Kura River near Gori. When Soso took off his shoes, another boy saw that the toes on Soso's foot were joined together rather than separated. He began to make fun of Soso, and called his foot "the devil's hoof." Soso smiled and pretended to laugh along with the teasing, but he refused to swim. Instead, he called Peradze away from the group and spoke quietly to him. Later, as the boy who had made fun of Soso walked home, Peradze attacked the boy and beat him savagely.

The name of the boy who made fun of Soso has been lost to history. Peradze's name is known because he recalled the incident many years later when he spoke about the powerful control that Soso had had over him and the other boys. The reason Peradze remembered the childhood event so well is that by the time his friend Soso Dzhugashvili was an adult, he had become the sole ruler of the Soviet Union. The world knew him as Joseph Stalin.

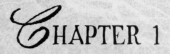

CHAPTER 1

BRUTAL BEGINNINGS

*J*oseph Stalin was one of the best-known villains in history, yet, strangely, he was also one of the least known. He was one of the twentieth century's most photographed leaders, and at the same time, one of the century's most mysterious men. There are two main reasons Stalin's life is a puzzle. First, there are no family records of his childhood – no diaries, letters, or photographs. He was born into poverty to parents who, like many Russian peasants, were illiterate.

Opposite: Joseph Stalin was the sole ruler of the Soviet Union for more than twenty years.

7

Another reason Stalin's life remains shadowy is that he ordered his biography, as well as the history of the Soviet Union, to be rewritten several times. With each of these rewrites, older records were destroyed. The more powerful Stalin became, the more he was able to take credit for things he had not done. His Communist biographers were forced to revise twentieth-century Russian history books to go along with Stalin's orders. The aim was to present to the world the most flawless possible account of the great leader. By the time Stalin was elderly, official Soviet history books claimed that he was the one man who had changed Russia from a backward society into an industrial superpower.

Although Stalin's childhood and early adult years were of great interest to many historians, research into his life was almost impossible before the Soviet Union collapsed in 1989. In that year, secret documents of the former Soviet Union were first opened to the public. Many of these documents had been compiled by early leaders of the Communist Party and hidden away—even from Stalin. The feared Soviet secret police, the KGB, had also kept information about Stalin, just as it had files on other leaders. The vast amount of material held information about Stalin's early life, and it provided many previously unknown details of Stalin's rise to power.

Childhood and Early Years

Joseph Stalin was born Iosif Vissarionovich Dzhugashvili on what most historians believe was December 21, 1879. He was born in the modern-day country of Georgia, which was then a part of the Russian Empire. Iosif is the Russian

Stalin's birthplace (above) was a tiny shoe repair shop in Gori, Georgia.

equivalent of "Joseph," Vissarionovich means "son of Vissarion," and Dzhugashvili was his last name. Throughout his childhood, he was known by the nickname "Soso," the Georgian equivalent of "Joey."

Stalin was born in the village of Gori, Georgia, which was located between the Black Sea and the Caspian Sea. Georgia was bordered by Russia to the north and the Black Sea to the east. Its western border was the province of Azerbaijan. To the south lay the province of Armenia and the country of Turkey. Georgia is a mountainous country. The Caucasus Mountains, which separated Russia from Georgia, presented a formidable obstacle to invading armies over the centuries. People who migrated into Russia from Georgia were often called Caucasians rather than Georgians.

Stalin was the only surviving child of parents who married in 1874. His three older brothers had all died in infancy. His father, Vissarion Dzhugashvili, was a shoemaker. His mother, Yekaterina, worked as a servant in well-to-do households. The family's native language was Georgian, which was the only language Stalin spoke until his school years, when he had to learn Russian, the language used in classes.

Stalin's father, nicknamed Beso, had grown up in a family that had a reputation for violence. Beso's father had participated in peasant revolts in Georgia and had served several terms in prison. Beso's older brother was stabbed to death in a drunken brawl. At his own wedding, rather than take part in the celebration, Beso got into a fistfight with one of his wife's relatives.

Beso and his wife, whose nickname was Keke, lived in a room about 15 feet square above his shoe repair shop. The close quarters and Beso's terrible temper—which was worse when he drank—led to frequent violence. From his earliest days, Stalin saw his father beat his mother. Stalin, too, was a victim of his father's rage. Several times, Keke told neighbors, her husband lifted Soso over his head and threw him to the floor.

Eventually, Stalin's father's drinking began to affect his strength and overall health. When he lashed out at his family, Stalin's mother began to fight back. Stalin witnessed many brawls between his parents. Finally, when his wife beat him unconscious in a fistfight, Beso left Gori and moved to the city of Tiflis to work in a shoe factory.

When Stalin's mother became the head of the household, she took out her bitterness about her situation on her son, and beat him savagely for any disobedience. Throughout the beatings, the young boy learned to absorb the punishment without tears. The violence and beatings in his home, however, affected Stalin's personality from his earliest years. A neighbor recalled that Stalin grew up as an "embittered, rude, stubborn child, with an intolerable character."

In September 1888, Stalin became a pupil at the Gori Church School, from which he graduated in 1894. As an adult, Stalin claimed to have been an honor student, yet it took him six years to complete what should have been a four-year program. There are two possible reasons for this discrepancy. First, Stalin contracted smallpox at some point during his childhood. Recuperation would have taken several months in those days, which would have set him back in his studies. He could have missed a year of school at that time.

The second reason for the discrepancy may have been his father. Vissarion did not want to pay the small fee required for his son's education. Instead, he wanted his son to come to Tiflis to learn the shoemaking business. On one visit home, he took his son out of school and brought him back to Tiflis to work with him in the factory. Apparently, Stalin remained with his father for almost a year before his mother came to Tiflis and forced Beso to allow the boy to return to school. By age 11, Stalin was back in school. It was at about that time that Beso was killed, as his brother had been, in a drunken brawl.

By age 15, Stalin had reached his full adult height of five feet, four inches.

Adolescence and Early Adult Years

By the time he reached early adolescence, Stalin had reached his full adult height of five feet, four inches. His face was severely scarred from smallpox. He also walked with a slight limp because he had been born with the toes of his left foot joined together. In spite of his size and slight disability, Stalin was physically fit and very strong.

In 1894, 15-year-old Stalin went to Tiflis to attend the Tiflis Theological Seminary, a secondary school that trained young men for the priesthood in the Russian Orthodox faith, Russia's official religion. Stalin's mother was determined to see her son continue his education, and to become a priest was the most respected career available to someone of his background. He won a partial scholarship to the seminary, and the remainder of his fees were paid by his mother and one of her employers.

At first, Stalin found his studies difficult. A law passed several years earlier required all lessons to be taught in Russian, and Stalin had not yet mastered the language, which was completely different from his native Georgian. In fact, throughout his life, he had a thick Georgian accent, and even after decades of practice, he often stumbled over Russian and was unable to express himself clearly.

Stalin arrived in Tiflis during a time when political unrest had gripped the country for more than 30 years. In 1861, peasants who had been ruled by the powerful czar and landholding nobles for three centuries were granted limited freedom by Czar Alexander II. This partial freedom made many peasants eager to win greater rights, and they began to join forces with young Russian political radicals who opposed rule by the wealthy aristocrats. Throughout the 1870s, revolts against the czar broke out across Russia. In 1881, a young member of a radical group known as the People's Will threw a bomb at Alexander II and killed him.

"A Nation of Slaves"

Few nations in nineteenth-century Europe were as politically and socially backward as Russia. The unchallenged and brutal rule of the Russian king—known as the czar—and his nobles resembled the government of a kingdom in the Middle Ages. Until 1861, landless peasants, known as serfs, were the property of landowning nobles. The leader of a peasant uprising in the late 1800s said that Russia was "a nation of slaves."

Peasants harvesting potatoes by hand was a common sight in nineteenth-century Russia.

In 1861, Alexander II faced growing unrest after Great Britain and France defeated Russia in a war. To appease the people, he granted limited rights to the serfs. Although serfs were not allowed to own land individually, groups of serfs could hold land in common. Village-sized organizations, which came to be called soviets, elected a spokesperson, a tax collector, and other officials to take responsibility for the welfare of the village. The peasants voted on taxes and on how money should be spent for the common good. The community organized work groups for public tasks, and the members were also responsible for the maintenance of public order and the way of life within the group.

The most important task of the community was the assignment of plots of land. Usually, assignments were made by a complicated system that divided land into multiple strips, which guaranteed families equal shares of both good and poor soil. The group periodically changed the distribution of land among households, due to changes in families, labor strength, and taxes.

This system of collective property governed by group decision-making was a basic form of government called socialism. The development of socialism on a small scale in the Russian countryside during the second half of the nineteenth century laid the foundation for a similar, but larger, state-controlled system that overthrew the last czar, Nicholas II, in 1917.

The czar's son, Alexander III, took power after his father's assassination and immediately began to reverse many of the reforms that his father had established, including the limited freedoms given to peasants. The Russian army rounded up and executed dozens of young men who had been involved in the assassination plot. Censorship of the press grew increasingly strict. The dreaded secret police began to kidnap, imprison, and execute people who spoke or wrote against the czar. Non-Russian minorities, especially Jews, were attacked by supporters of the czar. Hundreds of thousands of Jews were killed or driven

Czar Alexander II was assassinated by political radicals in 1881.

from Russia during a time that became known as the pogrom, a Hebrew word for "devastation."

The crackdown on political dissent during the reign of Alexander III actually helped build support for the most radical political parties. As the violence by the czar's forces increased, radicals began to secretly publish documents that called for a revolution against the czar.

One of the most widely read of these publications was a book called the *Revolutionary's Catechism* by

15

Sergei Nachaev. The book claimed that all of Russian society must be destroyed and a new nation built on the ruins. Nachaev said that for a true revolution to occur, revolutionaries must "unite with the savage world of the violent criminal." The majority of the population had to be exterminated, he claimed, because Russia was such a backward, medieval country.

With such revolutionary ideas, Nachaev and other radicals quickly became targets of the secret police. Many fled to a distant place where they felt the Russian government would be unlikely to follow them—the city of Tiflis, which was separated from the Russian heartland by the formidable Caucasus Mountains. Thus, the impressionable adolescent Stalin arrived in Tiflis at about the same time that the city became a gathering place for the most violent Russian political radicals.

In 1894, the year Stalin began his studies at the seminary in Tiflis, Alexander III died. His son, Nicholas II, took power and continued the strict rule of his father, which only increased the fury of the radicals and helped them gain support. At some point early in his education, Stalin

Czar Alexander III reversed many of his father's liberal policies toward peasants and minorities.

crossed paths with these young men, and a copy of the *Revolutionary's Catechism* fell into his hands.

Stalin had loved to read throughout his life. At a bookstore in Gori, he found and read popular literature by authors from Georgia. One book in particular grabbed his youthful imagination: *The Parricide* [Father Killer], by an author named Kazbegi. In the novel, a Georgian outlaw named Koba leads a band of mountain men against the czar. Koba became Stalin's role model, and after he read the *Revolutionary's Catechism*, Stalin began to call himself "Koba."

Young Radical

By the time Stalin enrolled in the Tiflis seminary, it had acquired a dubious reputation. Teachers were abusive to students, and students were hostile in return. In 1885, a student had struck the principal of the school. The next year, another student killed the principal, and the school was closed for a year. In 1890, there was a student strike. In 1893, students who did not want to learn Russian demanded a return to the study of Georgian. Eighty students were expelled for their demands.

Despite the seminary's reputation, Stalin was eager to excel in his studies. He fit in well with the other students and maintained high marks in his first year.

17

THE MARXIST PHILOSOPHY

For most of the nations of Europe, the 1800s were a time of enormous change. Perhaps the biggest change was the Industrial Revolution that led to economies that were based on factory labor rather than agriculture. Although some leaders of industry became wealthy during this period, millions more people worked in dirty, dangerous conditions for low wages. The enormous gap between rich and poor led to widespread revolts and protests against a system that took advantage of the labor of many to benefit a few.

In 1848, German social philosopher Karl Marx wrote a book titled *The Communist Manifesto* in which he explained his theories of history, economy, and the development of political systems. Marx believed that human history was a struggle for economic power between the ruling class, which he called the bourgeoisie, and the working class, which he called the proletariat. All societies, according to Marx, followed a three-

Karl Marx urged workers around the world to revolt against the wealthy, ruling classes.

point path of development. In the beginning, society is a feudal state, ruled by an aristocratic bourgeoisie and a proletariat of serfs. In this state, the aristocracy are landlords, and the workers are peasants. The serfs work the land for a living and, in return for that privilege, give part of their crops to the aristocracy. This enables the aristocracy to live entirely from the efforts of others and not have to perform any work of their own. The aristocracy owns everything, yet does nothing. The peasants own nothing, but do all the work. This is unfair, according to Marx.

The next stage in Marx's social philosophy is the capitalist stage. At this level, a class of tradespeople appears in the middle of society. This working class is the next level of proletariat. It is far better off than the serfs, but not nearly as well off as the aristocracy. The aristocracy in the second stage has been replaced by wealthy capitalists—called "bosses"—who control industries and equipment. In Marx's second stage, the bosses themselves do no work, but instead live from the efforts of the workers. The difference from the first stage is that the proletariat works for wages instead of on the land, so the workers make some profit. Also, the proletariat are mobile—they can move from job to job. In the second stage, there is also a class called the petit bourgeoisie. These are small capitalists who own stores, or farmers who own a small amount of land. The petit bourgeoisie are capitalists in that they own property, but they are in business for themselves and do all their own work. They do not take advantage of the workers.

According to Marx, the natural course of history will lead the proletariat to unite and bring about a revolution to depose rich capitalists. He called this stage three. In this stage, capitalists will lose their property and all the wealth they earned from others' labor. In order to make all things equal, Marx believed, all property, wealth, and possessions will be controlled by the state. Everyone will work for the state and receive equal compensation for their efforts—"from each according to his ability, to each according to his needs," as he explained. No one will be any richer or poorer than anyone else. This third stage is the perfect society, where all things and all people are equal.

Many of those who supported Marx believed that this revolution would happen among all workers as a natural and peaceful stage of human evolution. These people called themselves Socialists, a term that came into use at about the same time Marx wrote his book. Marx, however, believed that the revolution would not be peaceful, and that revolutionaries he called "Communists" would lead the struggle. Finally, he also believed that, in certain instances, it was possible to bypass stage two. Under the most oppressive conditions, such as those in nineteenth-century Russia, the serfs could unite and—led by Communists—bring about the revolution and move directly from stage one to stage three.

In his second year, however, concerns grew among the faculty about the influence of political radicals on the seminary students. Teachers began to spy on students and search their lockers for banned political writings. Stalin, like many of his fellow teenage students, rebelled against this intrusion on his privacy. The students smuggled more and more banned material into the school, and teachers were forced to confiscate it. Stalin was disciplined after he read to a group of students from banned books more than a dozen times during his second year. "I joined the revolutionary movement at 16," Stalin later said about these youthful activities.

It was during this time in his life, while he read banned books and discussed radical political ideas, that Stalin first read the works of Karl Marx. Several decades earlier, Marx, a German philosopher, had written a book titled *The Communist Manifesto*. In it, Marx predicted that the workers of the world would eventually rebel against capitalists—wealthy owners of business and industry—and create a worldwide, classless society. In such a society, all people would be equal. The government would own all business, industry, and agriculture, and would make all decisions in regard to the economy.

On a small scale, the collective decision-making used by Russian peasants was such a system. In other ways, however, Russia was too primitive to make Marx's worldwide workers' revolt a reality. Marx believed that workers would take power in a capitalist industrial economy. In the 1890s, Russia was far from an industrialized, capitalist society. Thus, although radicals and rebellious adolescents such as Stalin were persuaded by Marx's theories, they agreed that it could take years for a revolution to occur in Russia. To bring it about, they resolved to do all they could to weaken the czar's rule and pave the way for a society based on Marxist ideals.

In 1898, Stalin talked to a fellow radical at the seminary and announced that he intended to leave school to help start a workers' revolution. His companion urged him to remain in school for at least another year. The more education he received, the friend said, the more valuable he would be to the movement. At the end of the 1899 spring term, however, Stalin was expelled from the Tiflis Theological Seminary when he refused to take his final examinations. His political activities had taken too much time away from his studies to allow him to pass the exams.

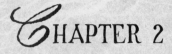

CHAPTER 2

EARLY BOLSHEVIK YEARS

By the beginning of the twentieth century, Russia was the largest country in the world. Its borders extended from the Baltic Sea in the west to the Pacific Ocean in the east, and as far south as China and Afghanistan. The czar ruled this enormous empire from the city of St. Petersburg on the Baltic Sea during the summer and from Moscow in western Russia during the winter. For centuries, the czars had ruled much as kings of Europe had ruled in the Middle Ages. They gave land grants—and power—to nobles who, in turn, ruled landless peasants called serfs who were little more than slaves. While many countries in western Europe became modern industrialized nations in the 1800s, Russia remained backward, and the majority of its people lived in extreme poverty.

In the 1890s, shortly after Nicholas II came to the throne, oil was discovered in southern Russia. Suddenly, Russia began to change from a nation of remote, widely scattered peasant villages to a nation with cities and industries. Peasants left the impoverished countryside to work in factories, oil fields, and other businesses. As industrialization grew, the ruling classes became fearful that they would lose their traditional hold on power. The czar and his supporters became more harsh and brutal than ever before. They passed strict laws, enforced by secret police, that limited workers' rights in the same way they had kept serfs in slavery for centuries.

In response to government policies, workers in many cities began to organize into local councils called soviets. The soviets used a system of collective decision-making and organized protests against the factory bosses. In 1898, many soviets across the country united to form the Russian Social Democratic Party (RSDRP), which was based on the traditional socialist ideas that formed the basis of the collective decision-making they had followed for several decades. Part of the membership of the RSDRP was also fiercely dedicated to the eventual overthrow of the czar.

Stalin's Only Job

On December 26, 1899, Stalin became an accountant at the Tiflis Observatory, where he worked nights. His job was to keep meteorological records for the area. He used his office as a place to hide banned political literature, and in his free time, he worked to organize a local chapter of the RSDRP.

In March 1901, police raided the observatory in search of banned RSDRP pamphlets and other illegal literature. They found none, but Stalin was fired because his employers did not want to be linked to a suspected member of the RSDRP. From that point on, Stalin never held another job. Instead, he devoted his life to revolution. Like many radicals, Stalin lived in tiny cellars or so-called safe houses, which were hiding places in which families carried on normal activities while they sheltered radicals. He carried forged identity papers in case he was stopped by police. He wore the same set of tattered clothes and lived on one small meal a day.

Most of those who became full-time revolutionaries understood that it was only a matter of time before they were arrested and sent into exile in a distant region of Russia. In some ways, imprisonment and exile became proof of dedication to the revolutionary cause, and those who were arrested were widely admired by other revolutionaries. For much of 1901, Stalin organized demonstrations, wrote articles on workers' rights under the pen name Koba, and distributed pamphlets.

Though Stalin (standing left) was not a powerful speaker, he built great support among the workers because of his dedication to Marxism.

As part of his work, Stalin also appeared before workers' groups to speak about the theories of Karl Marx. Though he was not as polished a speaker as other party members, his ungrammatical Russian, slow speech, and Georgian accent won Stalin many working-class admirers in Tiflis. This led some of Stalin's fellow radicals to claim that he hoped to bypass the collective rule of the party's committee and assert individual control.

The First Exile

Late in 1901, a warrant that charged Stalin with illegal political organization activities was issued by police in Tiflis, and the ruling committee of the RSDRP took advantage of the opportunity to send him away. He was sent to the Black Sea port of Batum, on the Georgian coast, where he helped organize a protest by workers against the local authorities. In early 1902, the large demonstration turned violent. Several police officers were injured, and 15 demonstrators were killed. Stalin, the main organizer, was not hurt, however. He had left the city before the demonstration to avoid capture.

In early April 1902, after he hid for a time in safe houses in the Caucasus Mountains, Stalin returned to Batum to resume his revolutionary activities. This time, the building in which he hid was surrounded by police, and he was arrested for his participation in the earlier demonstration. Stalin spent the next 18 months in the brutal Batum jail.

At first, Stalin was terrified to be behind bars. Living conditions were filthy, and the food was barely fit to eat. Beatings from guards were common, and the regular criminals in the jail also beat the political prisoners. Stalin fell into despair.

At a low point, however, Stalin recalled the words of the *Revolutionary's Catechism* that he had read at the seminary: "Ally yourself with the criminal world." As the penniless son of abusive parents, Stalin found that he had a great deal in common with the criminals, who came from similar backgrounds. Although he lacked physical strength and size, in one incident, he showed the most hardened criminals the toughness he had acquired in his earliest years as he fended off the fists of his parents.

One day, the guards decided to hand out an extra punishment to the political prisoners. The guards formed two long lines and forced the prisoners to walk between them. A prisoner later recalled, "Koba passed between the ranks, book in hand, refusing to bow his head under the rain of blows from rifle butts." The display of personal determination earned Stalin respect throughout the prison. He soon became the leader of all the prisoners and formed special bonds with the largest and most brutal inmates. Other inmates who refused to follow his directions suffered beatings at the hands of Stalin's companions.

Stalin Follows Lenin

During the months that Stalin was imprisoned, the RSDRP underwent a tremendous upheaval. The change occurred largely among the leaders of the party who lived in comfortable exile outside of Russia. Among those exiles, the unquestioned leader was Vladimir Lenin, who had escaped from Russia and fled to Brussels, Belgium, in early 1903. In July 1903, Lenin met a large group of Russian exiles—members of the RSDRP—to plan the next stage of their political action.

27

Although some exiles were satisfied to continue the current efforts to bring about a revolution in Russia, Lenin sought support for his ideas about the way the party should operate.

Instead of a loosely organized ruling committee, Lenin insisted on a committee in which one person was the leader and the other members were assigned lesser positions of authority. There would be no collective decision-making, Lenin said. The efforts of the RSDRP would no longer be directed toward the overthrow of the czar and the gradual development of state modeled after the ideas of Karl Marx. The immediate goal would be a complete revolution through violent means, led by a core group of professional revolutionaries.

At the end of the meeting, the majority of the members voted to support Lenin's views. The Russian word for "majority" is Bolshevik, and that is the name by which that wing of the RSDRP became known, despite the fact that in terms of total supporters, they were not a majority. Those who supported gradual reform were named after the Russian word for "minority"—*Menshevik*—although the number of supporters throughout the party was exactly opposite from its name.

Although he was thousands of miles away and knew nothing of the changes that had occurred, Stalin was familiar with Lenin and his ideas. At some point during his imprisonment, Stalin was given a book written by Lenin in early 1902 and titled *What Is to Be Done?* The book changed the course of Stalin's life. Before he read Lenin's work, Stalin believed that for a workers' revolution to take place, a capitalist society first had to replace the rule of the czar. Like most members of the RSDRP, Stalin believed his main goal was to build a foundation for future generations to carry out the revolution. He did not foresee a Marxist state in his lifetime. In his book, Lenin argued that a secret organization of professional revolutionaries could successfully create a revolution that would bypass the capitalist stage of development. For this to occur, Lenin believed, the majority of the population would have to be exterminated, simply because they were not advanced enough to understand the political process. Stalin immediately accepted Lenin's theory. The idea of bloodshed on an enormous scale did not concern him, as long as it brought the prospect of a revolution closer.

In October 1903, Russian authorities sentenced Stalin for his political activities. He was sentenced to three years of exile in Niznhnyaya Uda, a village in Siberia, the remote northern region of Russia. Under czarist rule, a person sentenced to exile was sent to an isolated village in

Political radicals sent to exile in Siberia lived in lonely desolation.

a remote area. The worse the crime, the more remote the village. The prisoner could board with a family in the village, live alone, or share quarters with fellow prisoners. Movement throughout the village was not strongly restricted, although exiles were not allowed inside certain businesses. Exiles were allowed to write letters and receive them from family and friends, although anything written could be read by authorities. Mail drop-offs and pick-ups occurred several times a year.

Exile villages were lightly guarded, and escape was fairly easy. Because Siberia was so remote, however, there were few roads and no railways. Thus, an exile who escaped often ended up thousands of miles from civilization with no way to get there. An exile who was caught was simply returned to the village to serve the rest of the sentence.

Stalin arrived at his assigned village in November 1903. He wore only a light coat in one of the coldest regions on earth. He immediately tried to escape, but frostbite on his nose and ears forced him to turn back. Once he recovered, Stalin escaped in early January 1904 with forged identity papers in case he was stopped. By February, he had made his way by reindeer sled and horse-drawn wagon back to Tiflis. There, he lived in a safe house with party member Sergei Alliluyev, his wife, Anna, and their four-year-old daughter, Nadya. For the next year, Stalin remained in hiding and edited a radical newspaper, the *Caucasian Workers' News Sheet.*

In 1905, Stalin was able to sneak across the Russian border to Finland to attend a convention of the newly formed Bolshevik wing of the RSDRP. It was there that he first met his idol, Lenin. Eight years older than Stalin, Lenin was the son of a Russian civil service official. He had grown up in relative comfort and had received a good education. At age 17, he had dedicated his life to revolution after he had witnessed the execution of his older brother. Lenin's brother was hanged for his participation in a plot to assassinate Czar Alexander III, the ruler whose father had been assassinated in 1881.

Lenin first began to organize workers in St. Petersburg. In 1895, he was exiled to Siberia, where he began to write his book, *What Is to Be Done?* Eventually, Lenin escaped from exile and fled Russia to finish his book and continue his political activities abroad.

In a speech during the Bolshevik meeting, Lenin stated that true revolutionaries should obtain funds for the revolution through illegal means, such as bank robberies, fraud, and other crimes against the wealthy. He called this the "expropriation" of resources for party use. Stalin fully supported this idea, which agreed with the beliefs expressed in the *Revolutionary's Catechism.* He discussed methods of expropriation with Lenin during their first meeting.

Although Stalin came from a background very different from Lenin's, the Bolshevik leader saw Stalin as an ideal revolutionary. This was not because Stalin was a brilliant political philosopher or inspiring speaker. Instead, it was because he was a dedicated radical who, like Lenin, had almost no interests other than revolution. When Lenin called for Bolsheviks

A police mug shot shows Stalin in the early 1900s.

to engage in "the murder of policemen and in arson," Stalin eagerly offered to assemble revolutionaries inside Russia for that purpose. Lenin gave Stalin his approval and sent him back to Tiflis with instructions to train young radicals in terror and expropriation.

War and Revolution

At the same time that the Bolsheviks were active outside of Russia, the country faced international problems on a much larger scale. These problems began in 1904, when Russian forces took control of Manchuria and Korea, two Asian regions that were rich in the iron ore and coal Russia needed for industrial growth. Japan expressed strong objections to Russian expansion. The Japanese, who also wanted the natural resources of the regions, offered to divide the area. The Russian government refused and warned the Japanese that any attempt to take Manchuria or Korea would result in war.

The czar and his ministers were confident that the Russian navy was powerful enough to defeat Japan. They also hoped that a show of force by the Russian military would serve as a threat to Russian political parties such as the RSDRP and make them back off in their demands for a change in government. In fact, the opposite happened.

In 1904, Japan staged a surprise attack at Port Arthur on the far eastern coast of Russia. Over the next year, a series of Japanese victories destroyed much of the Russian fleet in Asia. Russia withdrew from Korea and Manchuria, and the area fell under Japanese control.

The "Bloody Sunday" revolt of 1905 occurred when police shot a group of religious leaders who were leading a peaceful demonstration.

Although the terms of the peace treaty with Japan did not hurt Russia's reputation internationally, the defeat in what became known as the Russo-Japanese War showed that the empire was militarily weak. Political groups and workers' organizations did not fear the Russian military. Instead, they saw an opportunity to move toward a more democratic form of government.

In January 1905, Father Georgii Gapon, a Russian Orthodox priest who was the leader of a moderate workers' group, led a peaceful march in St. Petersburg to present a petition to the czar. The petition requested changes that would allow Russians a voice in the government. Nervous royal troops opened fire on the marchers and killed several hundred people. This event, called "Bloody Sunday," began the Revolution of 1905.

Soon after the incident in St. Petersburg, unions and political parties that supported democratic reforms organized workers' strikes, farmers' rebellions, army mutinies, and terrorist acts. Armed uprisings occurred in Moscow, St. Petersburg, and in the western area of Russia. Bolshevik fighters under Stalin and other leaders fought in Tiflis and in St. Petersburg.

In late 1905, Nicholas II issued the October Manifesto, which gave Russia its first constitution and promised all people civil liberties. The constitution established a Duma—a national legislature of representatives elected by voters. Those who agreed with this arrangement were called the Octobrists. Because they still hoped for a true revolution, the RSDRP and similar radical parties, such as the People's Will, refused to participate in the duma elections.

The formation of the duma did not end the violent tactics of the most radical groups. Bolshevik fighters became criminal gangs that continued to terrorize the areas in which they were strongest. Kidnappings, robberies, and murders by Bolshevik terrorists became common events in some places.

In 1906, Stalin organized and carried out the assassination of the military governor of Georgia. During the violence, Stalin's left arm was severely injured when a carriage rolled over it. For the rest of his life, his arm remained partially paralyzed.

Despite his injury, Stalin remained involved in terrorist activities in the Tiflis area. In 1907, he led a band of more than 50 men in a daylight attack that took place in the city square. There, the Bolsheviks surrounded two carriages that took money to a government bank. The terrorists threw bombs into the crowds and fired pistols wildly to create confusion. Then they took the money from the carriages and fled. Dozens of police officers and civilians were killed in the robbery.

By the end of the first decade of the twentieth century, many Russians thought of Bolsheviks as nothing more than criminals. Although many Bolshevik terrorists kept the money they stole, Stalin sent all of the money he expropriated to Lenin and his fellow exiles. While the Bolshevik exiles outside of Russia lived in comfort—and some Bolshevik thieves in Russia lived well—Stalin remained dedicated to a life of extreme poverty.

Soon after the robbery in Tiflis, Lenin sent word that Stalin should leave the area for a while to avoid capture. Stalin went to the oil fields around the city of Baku, where he continued his terrorist activities for several years.

It was during his time in Baku that Stalin married. The date of his marriage is not known. His wife was Yekaterina Svanidze, a Georgian who was not involved in politics, but whose brother was a dedicated Bolshevik. Stalin and his wife had a son, Yakov, but little is known of Yekaterina, who is believed to have died around 1910. Stalin, who left his son to be raised by his wife's relatives, was fond of his wife. At her funeral, he remarked to a Bolshevik comrade, "She softened my stony heart. She is dead, and with her have died my last warm feelings for all human beings."

Shortly after his wife's death, Stalin was again arrested for political activities and sentenced to three years in exile. Over the next two years, he escaped and was recaptured twice. In 1912, he was able to escape from Russia entirely and traveled to Vienna, Austria, with the help of forged documents. There, Stalin met with Lenin and the Bolshevik exiles.

Shortly before Stalin's arrival, Lenin had arranged a meeting of Bolsheviks who lived outside of Russia. At the conference, he had claimed that the Bolsheviks were

Stalin wrote a number of articles and editorials for the party newspaper, Pravda.

the only true members of the RSDRP. The Mensheviks were thrown out. The Mensheviks protested, but they had no leader who commanded the kind of respect that Lenin did.

When Stalin met with Lenin, the debate over the exclusion of the Mensheviks was at its height. Stalin decided to write a long article for the party newspaper in which he explained that Lenin's path was the most direct way to achieve a worldwide revolution. "Bloody Marxism," he wrote, was the way to victory. He signed the article "Stalin," the Russian term for "man of steel." He used that name for the rest of his life.

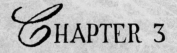
REVOLUTION AND CIVIL WAR

*S*oon after their meeting in Vienna, Lenin sent Stalin to St. Petersburg to organize fighters. It was more difficult to hide in the Russian capital than it was in a city such as Tiflis, and Stalin was arrested for his membership in a banned political party soon after he arrived in 1913. This time, the authorities decided to send Stalin to the farthest, most desolate region of Siberia. He was sentenced to five years of exile in the tiny settlement of Kureika, inside the Arctic Circle.

Stalin sank into despair as he endured daily winter temperatures of -20° F. He wrote letters to friends in St. Petersburg in which he begged for money. "I've got no provisions. . . . I must have firewood . . . but there's no money. I did have money but it all went to warm clothing. Twenty or thirty rubles would be a real life-saver," he wrote.

The next four years were the darkest of Stalin's life. Although he did receive some funds, he was in too remote a region to even attempt an escape. He spent whole days in bed, with his face to the wall. He felt as though his dedication to the Bolsheviks had amounted to nothing.

World War I

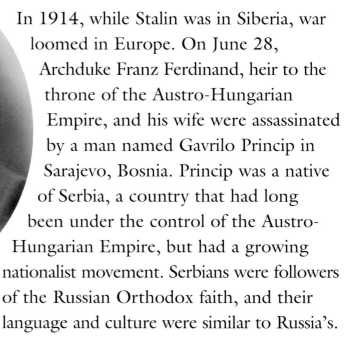

Archduke Franz Ferdinand was assassinated in 1914.

In 1914, while Stalin was in Siberia, war loomed in Europe. On June 28, Archduke Franz Ferdinand, heir to the throne of the Austro-Hungarian Empire, and his wife were assassinated by a man named Gavrilo Princip in Sarajevo, Bosnia. Princip was a native of Serbia, a country that had long been under the control of the Austro-Hungarian Empire, but had a growing nationalist movement. Serbians were followers of the Russian Orthodox faith, and their language and culture were similar to Russia's.

The assassination set a number of events into motion that rapidly grew violent because of the tangled alliances among European nations. In July, Austria-Hungary attacked Belgrade, the Serbian capital. Russia then entered the war to defend Serbia. That action drew Germany, an ally of Austria-Hungary, into the conflict. At that time, France was an ally of Russia. Germany, which was located between France and Russia, declared war on France. That led England to join France in a declaration of war against Germany and its allies. By mid-August 1914, World War I had begun.

At the outbreak of the fighting, people on both sides were confident that the war would end quickly. It lasted four years, however, and the clash of traditional nineteenth-century concepts of warfare and modern twentieth-century weapons caused the number of troops killed in the war to reach numbers far beyond those of any earlier conflict.

Although Russia had entered the war in its first weeks, the country was unprepared for a fight on such a huge scale. Russia had just begun to recover from its losses to Japan, and it was both militarily and industrially weak compared with other nations in the war. During 1915 and 1916, Russian troops suffered several defeats, and soon Russia was on the verge of collapse.

Food riots in St. Petersburg were broken up when the czar's troops fired on angry peasants.

Short of troops, the government decided to draft all exiles for military service. Stalin was taken to the city of Krasnoyarsk to join the military in December 1916. Because he walked with a limp and had a semiparalyzed arm, however, he was found unfit for duty and sent to the village of Achinsk to complete his exile.

Meanwhile, thousands of miles away in St. Petersburg, the Russian people were near revolt. Defeats in battle, food shortages, and a brutally cold winter led to conditions that the Bolsheviks could use to their advantage. By late February, there were food riots in the streets. Soon, radicals took over the city jails and forced the guards to free all the prisoners. Then the jail was set on fire. Troops were ordered to fire on the demonstrators, but they refused. On March 2, 1917, Nicholas II stepped down from the throne. After 300 years, Russia was no longer under czarist rule.

When Stalin received word that the czar had stepped down, he immediately set out for St. Petersburg. When he arrived on March 12, a temporary government set up by the duma was at work to try to negotiate with the workers' groups—the soviets—that had been behind the revolt. Duma officials called for a return to order and promised reforms that would guarantee greater rights for workers. The duma, however, was unwilling to go along with the most pressing demand of the soviets—immediate withdrawal from the war. For the next nine months, the duma government tried to balance the demands of the soviets with its commitment to its allies in the war.

Once in St. Petersburg, Stalin became the editor of the Bolshevik Party's newspaper, *Pravda*—the Russian word for "truth." At first, Stalin wrote editorials that advocated cooperation between the Bolsheviks and the duma government. Stalin's attitude, along with that of most Bolsheviks, changed when Lenin returned to Russia in April.

Lenin immediately condemned the duma and said that it was a capitalist institution. True freedom, he said, could only come about with the overthrow of all capitalists everywhere. Stalin quickly altered his *Pravda* editorials and became one of Lenin's chief aides.

43

A bloody civil war brought troops from the czar's White army (above) from the German front to fight the Communist Red army.

By the end of August, the duma's attempts to balance the demands of the army at war and the restless soviets at home led to a bitter disagreement between the head of duma and the head of the army, who wanted to disband the soviets. In September, when German forces seized several islands in the Baltic Sea and prepared to invade Russia, the army was torn between whether it should defend the Russian borders or handle the situation in the capital. News of a possible German attack on St. Petersburg caused government leaders to abandon the city. Russians took to the streets and began to loot the homes of wealthy residents who had fled.

During the time of turmoil, Bolsheviks had attempted to take control of soviets in Russia's largest cities. By early October, they took over the St. Petersburg soviet.

44

This drew a large force of Russian soldiers from the war front into St. Petersburg to force that city's soviet to disband. These troops, called the White army, were defeated by Bolsheviks and deserters from the regular army—whose combined force became known as the Red army. On October 25, 1917, the Red army stormed the Winter Palace, once the czar's residence, and seized power. The Bolsheviks then disbanded the duma government.

Through the months of upheaval, Stalin remained a close aide and confidant of Lenin, who was the

Europe 1919
Borders after
World War I

The Red army was made up of militarily inexperienced men and women who believed in Communist principles.

unquestioned leader of the Bolsheviks. Now, at last in power, the first priority of the new Bolshevik government was to end the war with Germany. The White army was by now almost nonexistent. Lenin knew that the country desperately needed to solve its severe economic problems. In order to accomplish this, the Russians signed a peace treaty with Germany on March 3, 1918. Russia became a nation ruled by revolutionaries who had strong support in the cities among workers, but who were almost unknown across the vast rural expanses of the country. To affirm their commitment to the Marxist ideal of worldwide revolution, the Bolsheviks changed their name to the Communist Party. The name

"Communists" implied that they would work as a group to lead the country to the ideal worldwide Socialist society, the one envisioned by Marx.

The country over which the Communist Party claimed power quickly fell into chaos. Although the Bolsheviks held power in the cities of Moscow and St. Petersburg, huge areas of Russia were torn by terrorists, czarist troops who had fled the cities, and common criminals. Revolts broke out in areas of southern Russia that preferred a czarist system to the rule of the former Bolshevik criminals and terrorists. Russians in the cities faced starvation. Lenin realized that he needed to send troops to the areas of conflict and to use them in the cities to control the mobs. The Red army, however, was largely an undisciplined group of radicals with no military experience.

To solve the most immediate problems, Lenin put the Red army under the control of Leon Trotsky, one of the intellectual leaders of the revolution. Trotsky declared that any soldier who disobeyed even the simplest order would be executed.

Leon Trotsky was one of the main political philosophers of the Communist Party.

Hundreds of soldiers were shot in the first months of Communist control, before the army became a more organized fighting force.

Lenin next assigned Stalin to lead a group of troops into the countryside to take grain forcibly from the peasants and send it to the cities. In May 1918, Stalin went to Tsaritsyn, the main Bolshevik outpost in northern Georgia. He set up a command post on a railway car and began a bloody wave of executions. He ordered his troops to shoot anybody who attempted to sell grain rather than surrender it. Anyone who did anything to imply that grain should not be sent to St. Petersburg was also shot—along with anyone in that person's family over the age of 12.

The killings took place largely after sunset. There were so many executions that Stalin ordered trucks around his rail car to run their engines at night to drown out the noise of the shots and the victims' screams. Bodies were stuffed into burlap bags and buried in a common grave. Each day, families of those who were missing came to the grave to dig up their loved ones for reburial.

The Russians who refused to give up their grain without payment were largely from the villages that had managed their cropland most successfully. These people, known as the kulaks, had briefly profited from the sale of their grain while the duma was in power. They had realized the rewards of a capitalist system and were unwilling to give away the grain they had worked so hard to raise. To force the kulaks to give up their grain, Stalin gave the poor—that is, the laziest and most hostile peasants—local control. They were given weapons and sent into the countryside to take the kulaks' grain.

Stalin's brutality brought results that pleased Lenin. As the executions and confiscation of grain took place, Stalin wrote to Lenin, "Our hand will not tremble. Our enemies will learn what enemies are. We shall spare nobody, and will give you the grain whatever happens."

By mid-summer, wagonloads of grain were on the way from Tsaritsyn to the starving people of St. Petersburg and Moscow. There were enormous numbers of deaths during this time of the so-called "Red Terror," and Lenin knew that many Bolsheviks felt uneasy about the murder of their fellow Russians. Stalin, Lenin realized, had no misgivings at all. He seemed naturally cruel—and he was devoted to Lenin's vision of world revolution.

During the bloody summer of 1918, Stalin renewed the acquaintance with the Alliluyev family, in whose home he had hidden when he returned to Tiflis from exile in 1904. They had come to Tsaritsyn from Tiflis to assist the Communist effort. Nadya, the daughter, was now 18 years old, and Stalin, nearly 40, found her attractive. For her part, Nadya was captivated by Stalin's ruthless revolutionary image. She saw marriage to him as a noble way to devote herself to the Bolshevik cause. By the end of the summer, they were husband and wife—after the revolution, no marriage ceremony was necessary. The couple had two children—a son, Vasily, born in 1921, and a daughter, Svetlana, born in 1926.

The New Economic Plan

For three years, from 1918 to 1921, civil war raged across Russia. Millions died while Lenin attempted to force his system into existence by brute force with tactics—such as those used by Stalin—that he called "war communism." Throughout those bloody years, Stalin continued to make a name for himself among the Communist leadership with merciless campaigns, first in Tsaritsyn, then in other areas of Russia.

Although Lenin admired Stalin's ruthlessness, other party intellectuals saw Stalin as a common peasant and a non-Russian foreigner. In a way, that perception was accurate. Stalin acknowledged his difference from the party founders and was proud of his working class—or proletariat—roots. His pride helped him dedicate himself to the cause of world revolution. Once he set a goal, such as the seizure of grain from farms, he did everything in his power to achieve it. He never doubted his abilities, and he never changed his mind. He could exert pressure to get things done and force others to comply with his will.

In 1921, after three years of bloodshed, Lenin finally abandoned war communism in favor of what he called the "New Economic Policy" (NEP). The slaughter in Russia had been condemned by countries around the world. Lenin knew that to build a Communist Russia on the ruins of the destroyed nation, he would have to restore, at least temporarily, a free capitalist market. It was the only way Russia could trade with other nations for the goods it desperately needed.

Despite the objections of longtime Bolsheviks, Lenin decided to postpone hard-line Marxism until the country had recovered from the effects of seven years of war. He also planned to weed out the older party members, and to strengthen his hold on the government, he would recruit younger people into the party.

Lenin took firm control through the establishment of the Cheka, a secret police unit that had unlimited powers. Cheka agents were given the right to shoot any Russian without question. Freedom of speech and political organization were abolished. At the same time that

Starving peasants wait in line for food handouts from international aid organizations.

Lenin presented the NEP to the outside world and to Russians who supported capitalism, he violated his original aims of collective rule by the people as he solidified his power. It was a lesson that Stalin learned to follow as he grew closer to Lenin.

To silence criticism within the party, Lenin created the position of general secretary of the Politburo, the body that governed the party and the nation. To fill the new post, he brought in the one person he felt he could trust to enforce party discipline—Stalin. By 1922, Stalin had the sole power to appoint local party officials anywhere in the country. Although he had little to do with the party members who debated the proper goals for a workers' revolution, the organization of the party—down to the smallest detail—was in his hands. While the Cheka crushed any remaining embers of revolt by the peasants, workers, and the old military, Stalin built a party that supported Lenin—and, by association, Stalin as well.

Even with the war over and the NEP in place, the people with the least power, the peasants, continued to suffer. Lenin took food from farms for industrial workers and the government. Food requisitioning—the seizure of food from the peasants who grew it—made the country's already severe food shortage a much larger problem. Despite aid from Western nations, 5 million Russian people starved to death in 1922.

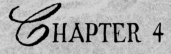

CHAPTER 4

RISE TO POWER

$\mathcal{O}$ne of Stalin's first accomplishments as general secretary was to force the ruling council of Communists to change the name of the country from Russia to the Union of Soviet Socialist Republics (USSR), which became known as the Soviet Union. Just six weeks after this change, on May 25, 1922, Lenin suffered the first of a series of strokes. Over the next two years, his health gradually grew worse.

The long period of Lenin's decline gave his potential successors time to put themselves in position to take over the party and the country. At that time, there were five major leaders of the Communist

Stalin (left) rose to power over (left to right) Alexei Rykov, Lev Kamenev, and Grigori Zinoviev.

Party, in addition to Stalin: Trotsky, Grigori Zinoviev, Lev Kamenev, Nikolai Bukharin, and Alexei Rykov. Stalin, however, was closest to Lenin and he obtained the responsibility for the supervision of Lenin's medical care. This made it possible for Stalin to control access to Lenin's bedside. He also controlled what government papers Lenin did or did not see.

As his health continued to fail, Lenin sensed that he would die soon and wrote extensive notes about who his successor should be. Two passages in particular

Stalin and Lenin (left) pose together in the early 1920s before Lenin suffered health problems.

referred to Stalin, whom Lenin observed on a regular basis during his long illness. Lenin called Stalin and Trotsky the two most able leaders of the Central Committee, the main governing body of the Communist Party. He then went on to say:

Stalin, having become General Secretary, has unlimited authority concentrated in his hands, and I am not sure whether he will be capable of using that authority with sufficient caution.

A later passage read:

Stalin is too rude, and this defect, though quite tolerable in our midst and in dealings among us Communists, becomes intolerable in a General Secretary. This is why I suggest that the comrades think about a way to remove Stalin from that post and appoint another man who in all respects differs from Comrade Stalin in his superiority—that is, more loyal, more courteous, and more considerate of comrades.

Lenin (right) met with leaders of worker organizations, but he usually felt more comfortable at political rallies and left such meetings to Stalin.

Lenin gave these notes, called his "Testament," to his wife. They were to be handed over to the party leadership upon his death. He suffered a final stroke on March 7, 1923, which left him incapacitated. He died on January 21, 1924. In his honor, the city of St. Petersburg was renamed Leningrad.

Shortly after Lenin's death, the "Testament" was read aloud at a Central Committee meeting. Stalin sat and listened in stunned silence. If Lenin had been alive to read those words, Stalin's career might have been finished. As it was, however, Stalin was saved by several factors. As general secretary, he had been able to recruit a large number of less-educated party members who had working-class backgrounds similar to his own. These new members admired Stalin because he was not a slave to idealistic theories. The other leaders came from the educated classes and often considered theory more important than practical application. Thus, when Stalin submitted his resignation, it was rejected by majority of the party.

Stalin was also saved by his supreme organizational skills. He knew how to maneuver people into alliances with each other and against other groups. He had done this even in childhood, and he had been a master of such practical politics since his earliest days. Even when it seemed that Lenin's negative remarks should have ended his career, Stalin was able to secure enough support to save himself.

Stalin, who had never been a fiery speaker or a magnetic leader like Lenin, was well suited for the backroom politics necessary in a one-party government. Although he was a brutal man, he projected an image of modesty, calm, and patriotism that was widely respected. As the power of the Communist Party became absolute, millions of Russians fell in line with the person who seemed to embody a concern for the welfare of the workers. That man was Stalin.

Socialism in One Country

After Lenin's death, the main debate in the Communist Party was over idealism versus practicality. The first issue to arise was whether to continue Lenin's economic plan. A number of Communists felt that if the plan remained in place too long, capitalism would take root in the country and would set back the path to world revolution. More practical party members insisted that the plan be continued to help Russians rebuild their lives.

Another debate centered on the concept that came to be called "socialism in one country." In December 1924, Stalin began to speak in favor of this idea. It went against the Marxist philosophy that called for a worldwide revolution, where the workers would take over the whole world together in one massive revolt. Stalin suggested that rather than wait for revolution to occur around the world, the Soviet Union should begin nationalization within its own borders and serve as a model for workers in other countries.

Stalin's opinion differed from those of his rivals for power. His most powerful opponent was Trotsky, who had been Lenin's companion since the RSDRP began. He was a well-respected figure, but was always an outsider because of his formidable intelligence and the fact that he was the only Jew among the top Bolsheviks. Jews in Russia, no matter what their political beliefs, had been targets of prejudice for decades. The country had a brutal history of anti-Semitic violence, and Stalin himself made anti-Semitic statements in private throughout his life.

Although Trotsky was never totally accepted, his main strength was that Lenin had regarded him as a political genius. Trotsky and Lenin were both Marxist idealists. The revolution should be worldwide, they believed, with no class systems left anywhere. Trotsky, however, had been practical enough to agree with the NEP that Lenin had adopted in 1921 after the civil war. He agreed that nationalization should be put off until the country recovered. By that time, he believed, workers around the world would follow Russia's example, and capitalism would fall.

Stalin's rivals Zinoviev and Kamenev believed—like Lenin and Trotsky—that all class systems should be abolished. They also believed that the majority of the peasant population should be forced to move off the land to help industrialize the country. Those who should become part of the labor force would be selected by local party leaders. Those who remained should be forced onto collective farms to raise food. Peasants must be used for the good of everybody, Zinoviev and Kamenev said.

They did not agree with Lenin's economic plan.

They thought the nationalization and collectivization policy should have been forced through, no matter what lives it might have cost. Both men were original Bolsheviks, and they drew a great deal of support from other older members. They also had a great deal of support in the cities.

Stalin's opponents Bukharin and Rykov, on the other hand, believed that it would take time to create a true proletarian state. They had the support of many Russians in rural areas, but overall, they were not as powerful as Zinoviev and Kamenev.

Although Stalin's rivals for power had played important roles in the formation of the Bolshevik movement and in the revolution, they lacked Stalin's brutal nature. It was that aspect of his personality that had appealed to Lenin at first, and it helped cause the downfall of the men who hoped to lead the Soviet Union. Throughout the years after Lenin's death, Stalin used his influence inside the party to put each of his rivals in a bad light. He played each against the others, and remained behind the scenes while they criticized each other. As he did so, Stalin created the impression that only he could carry on Lenin's work—and the party came to believe him.

In 1926, Trotsky was voted off of the central committee. Kamenev was expelled from the party.

A year later, in November 1927, Trotsky and Zinoviev were also expelled from the party. In 1928, Trotsky was sent into exile in Siberia, along with his followers. A year later, he was deported from the Soviet Union.

Stalin then turned on Bukharin and Rykov. In speeches and *Pravda* editorials, he accused them of impractical idealism and failure to support the concept of socialism in one country. By late 1928, he had built enough support to oust these rivals from important party positions. When he did this, he eliminated all his opposition. The poor son of a shoemaker, who had been ridiculed by his opponents for his lack of intelligence, now controlled the Communist Party and the Soviet Union.

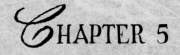

DECADE
OF DEATH

$\mathcal{A}$lthough the nation that Stalin led in 1930 was called the Soviet Union, in many ways, it remained the same backward Russian nation that it had been for centuries. It was a land of enormous natural resources but little industry. It was the largest country in the world, yet it had few roads, rail lines, or waterways, so travel was extremely difficult. The vast plains of central Russia were ideal for agriculture, but farming methods were primitive.

Between 1928 and 1930, while Stalin consolidated his control over the party, he came to realize that Lenin's NEP had produced unfortunate results for the Communists. Capitalism had the support of many Russians, especially the peasants, who were free to earn a profit on their work for the first time. Stalin knew that capitalism and free peasants would bring an end to the Communist state. What was needed, he felt, was a return to the terror of "war communism."

As the 1920s came to an end, Stalin announced his own plan for the nation. He discarded Lenin's economic plan and instead turned his attention to a transformation of the Soviet Union into an industrial superpower. He planned to accomplish this task with a return to nationalization and collectivization. Lenin had turned away from those aspects of communism because he had been alarmed at the loss of life during the civil war. Stalin had no such concerns. He did not care how many people died, as long as the nation prospered. "If one person dies, that is a tragedy," he said. "If a million people die, that is a statistic."

To return to the principles of the revolution, Stalin developed a five-year plan modeled after then-current business practices. The plan contained specific—and impossibly high—goals for industrial and agricultural production. The industrial output of the country was supposed to triple within five years, according to Stalin. Peasants would be moved from their traditional villages to state-run collective farms, where they would be forced to produce more wheat than ever before in Russia's long agricultural history.

When the first five-year plan began in 1929, Communist officials discovered that peasants were no more willing to leave their land and join government-owned collective farms than they had been ten years earlier. They were also every bit as willing to fight for their rights as they had been then. What was needed, Stalin believed, was a return to terror. He created a new secret police force, the NKVD, to replace the Cheka. He then turned his full fury on the one group of Russians who were most resistant to his plan—the most successful peasants, the kulaks.

In 1930, Stalin began a program of forced resettlement of kulak families. Kulaks were identified, as they had been in Tsaritsyn, by the less successful villagers in an area. Stalin said it was the patriotic duty of all true revolutionaries to point out the kulaks for the NKVD.

Throughout the bitter Russian winter of 1930–1931, more than 200,000 families were uprooted and transported to the coldest regions of Siberia. Originally, unheated huts were supposed to have been built to house the families. When Stalin received word that the huts were not finished, he gave the order to carry out the resettlement

Kulaks, the most successful farmers, became targets of Stalin during his first years in power.

anyway. Thousands of men, women, and children froze to death on the open plains of Siberia.

Stalin also turned to cities in search of those he called "wreckers," people who did not support his plan. In the city of Shakhty, the NKVD reported that skilled engineers were involved in sabotage of the city's efforts at industrialization. The engineers were not Communists, and Stalin immediately saw an opportunity to increase his power over the nation's industry. He publicly announced that, as capitalists, these men could not be trusted. Only Communists could be trusted in any area of supervision. This opened the way to replace all educated and trained workers left over from pre-revolutionary days with loyal party members.

Stalin had more than 50 engineers transported to Moscow for public trial. The press printed false accusations against them. They were tortured until they signed confessions that said they were "counterrevolutionaries." In the end, six engineers were sentenced to death, and the others received prison terms.

Meanwhile, the Communists proceeded with their plan to set up collective farms for the peasants who had not been sent to cities or to Siberia. During the first years of the five-year plan, Stalin's government removed 15 million peasants from their villages. About 13 million were sent to the cities to work in factories. About 2 million were sent to collective farms. Much of the forced collectivization took place in the large agricultural region that is the modern-day country of Ukraine.

In August 1932, Stalin wrote and put into effect a law entitled "On the Safeguarding of State Property." This law stated that all land, all growing crops, all harvested crops, all seed stock, all cattle, machinery,

Posters that encouraged workers to meet the goals of the five-year plan were displayed across Soviet cities.

equipment, and buildings belonged the Soviet government. Any attempt by peasants to use state property for their own benefit was punishable by death. Stalin personally ordered that no pardons be granted for these offenses.

Stalin's next step was to set the amount of wheat each peasant was required to grow for the state. Before the crop was planted, the government figured the maximum potential yield for each acre. Based on those figures, the government then told the peasants how much of that year's crop would be taken to feed people in the cities or be sold abroad to buy equipment needed to turn the Soviet Union into a powerful industrial nation.

While large, state-run farms were created in agricultural regions, industrial development was pushed at an impossible rate. All factory production was geared to turn out products such as tractors and mechanized equipment. The peasants, who labored to feed the entire nation, were only allowed to keep what was left after the government and industry had taken their share. The government, however, had figured the maximum yield at impossibly high rates. When the harvest was over, NKVD agents went to the collective farms to take the entire crop away to the cities.

Peasants were left with nothing. Thousands were sentenced to death if they stole a few ears of corn, took ten onions, or hid leftover wheat from the fields after the harvest had been completed. This became known among the people as the "law of five," a reference to the number of stolen ears of corn that could lead to execution. Children as young as 12 were shot or hanged for violations of the law.

Terror ruled the countryside. NKVD agents dug up the peasants' gardens and tore apart their houses to look for hidden stores of grain. Whatever they found, they took. As winter came on, the peasants were left with no food whatsoever.

Word of the famine reached other countries, and members of the U.S. State Department went to the region to learn whether the rumors were true. They discovered that conditions were actually worse than they had been told. Part of the report the Americans sent to the White House stated:

> *Conditions in the Ukraine are as follows. There is literally no bread there; no potatoes, no meat, no sugar—in a word, nothing of the basic necessities of life. All cats and dogs have disappeared, having perished or been eaten by hungry farmers. People*

"A Comrade Dear to Us"

Nadya Stalin was 22 years younger than Stalin.

In 1932, Stalin requested that Nadya accompany him to a dinner for party leaders. This was a rare occurrence; Stalin normally attended social events alone. During the dinner, Stalin drank heavily and threw cigarette butts and orange peels at his wife. He then addressed her as "Hey, you."

Nadya left the party in tears and returned to the family's apartment. There, she locked herself in her room and killed herself with a pistol Stalin had given her for protection.

Stalin was grief-stricken, but he had the presence of mind to make certain that the cause of his wife's death remained a secret. The government newspaper announced only that "a comrade dear to us" had died, and mentioned no cause of death. Thousands lined the streets for Nadya's funeral. Many believed they saw Stalin walk behind his wife's coffin to the cemetery. In fact, it was a Stalin look-alike. Stalin did not want to appear in public and risk assassination.

Throughout his rise to power and his brutal treatment of other Russians, Stalin's wife, Nadya, remained loyal and supportive of him. Although they argued frequently, Stalin never physically abused his wife, as his father had done to his mother. He was, however, a gruff, unsentimental man.

have also consumed all the field mice and frogs they could obtain. The only food most of the people can afford is a simple soup prepared of water and various weeds. The soup has no nutritive value whatever, and people remaining on such a diet get first swollen limbs and faces, which makes them appear like some dreadful caricature [cartoon image] of human beings. Then they gradually turn into living skeletons, and finally drop dead wherever they stand. The dead bodies are held at the morgue until they number fifty or more, and then are buried in mass graves. Worst of all, there is no escape from this hell on earth, as no one can obtain permission to leave the boundaries of the Ukraine.

The spring of 1933 was silent and barren in Ukraine. The birds and insects had been eaten by the starving population. Buds and fruits were stripped from trees long before they had a chance to ripen. More than 7 million people, one quarter of the population of Ukraine, died.

The Show Trials

By 1934, Stalin had crushed capitalism in the Soviet Union. In the cities, government-controlled newspapers printed countless stories about the success of the five-year plan that praised Stalin's heroic leadership. In fact, the plan was a failure, but the endless stream of propaganda convinced most Russians that it had worked. At the same time, people knew that if they expressed even the slightest doubt, the NKVD might appear at their door.

With farms collectivized and industry under government management, Stalin realized that he had no opposition. Russians, especially those in the cities who accepted the party's propaganda, felt as though a type of normalcy had settled over the Soviet Union. Party loyalists began to argue that Stalin should be moved into a more ceremonial post that was visible but less powerful. They felt the position of general secretary should go to Sergei Kirov, a Georgian and close friend of Stalin, who strongly supported the original Marxist ideal of collective decision-making.

Stalin knew that his power was threatened when he had no enemy to blame for any problems. First he had blamed the kulaks. Then it was the wreckers. Now it became the "old Bolsheviks." To arouse public opinion against traditional party leaders, Stalin decided that Kirov had to die. There is no trail of evidence, but many historians believe that Stalin approached the head of the secret police and told him that Kirov was an enemy agent. The

Stalin helped to carry the coffin of Kirov—the man he had ordered assassinated.

police chief hired an assassin, and Kirov was shot in a dark hallway outside his office on December 1, 1934.

As news of the murder reached the public, Stalin pretended to be outraged. He paid full honor to Kirov and gave him a state funeral. Then he drafted an emergency decree on terrorism, which placed the blame for Kirov's death on "old Bolsheviks" who were counterrevolutionaries. Another wave of terror began.

Anyone named as a counterrevolutionary terrorist was tried as quickly as possible and executed without any chance for an appeal. Bodies were cremated immediately and the ashes dumped in pits near NKVD headquarters. Stalin's murderous path now pointed in the direction of his former rivals. Some of Zinoviev's supporters were named as part of a center of terrorist activity and were arrested and shot. Families of the old Bolsheviks were shot or imprisoned. Zinoviev and

Kamenev, along with many of their supporters, were sentenced to jail terms and eventually shot. Stalin had ushered in a level of state-controlled terror that was worse than any period under the czars.

No one was safe from the terror—not family, friends, relatives, longtime associates, or even loyal supporters. Anyone who could possibly threaten Stalin's absolute power was falsely accused of a crime and arrested. Once a person was convicted, any relative or friends of that person suffered a similar fate.

Fear ruled the people's lives. Party members were arrested and charged with treason if they did not clap at Stalin's speeches. Newspaper editors were arrested for misprints that did not reflect what Stalin considered the true statistics of the five-year plan. Trials were held both in secret and in public, and they became a source of entertainment for average workers who believed that Stalin protected the revolution from old Bolsheviks.

In 1937, Bukharin, Rykov and all their supporters were charged with treason. Bukharin was even accused of a plot to kill Lenin 15 years earlier. Stalin told Bukharin personally that if he pled guilty, Stalin would see to it that his life was spared. At the end of the trial in which Bukharin did plead guilty, Stalin got up, called for the death penalty, and signed the death warrant.

"THE NEW CZAR"

One of the few people who did not fear Stalin in the 1930s was his mother, Yekaterina. Stalin arranged for his elderly mother to have an apartment in Tiflis where she could live out her final years. In 1936, when she was in her late seventies, her son made a visit to Tiflis. The visit was reported by the state newspaper as one in which Stalin's mother spoke proudly of her son. "The whole world rejoices when it looks upon my son and our country," she was reported to have said.

In fact, the meeting between mother and son was brief. Their conversation was very different from what was reported in the press.

Stalin's mother wanted her son to become a priest.

"Joseph, what exactly are you now?" she asked him.

"Do you remember the czar?" he answered. "I'm something like the czar."

"You'd have done better to become a priest," she said.

When his mother died a short time after the visit, Stalin did not attend the funeral. As with his wife's funeral, he did not want to risk assassination with a public appearance.

In all, more than half of the party membership and more than 70 percent of the Central Committee were executed between 1934 and 1937. Stalin personally signed more than 230,000 death warrants—and those were only the ones he thought were important enough for him to deal with personally. Almost all military leaders were eliminated, along with a large percentage of the secret police.

As a result of the enormous number of executions, railway yards had no qualified personnel left, and factories had no trained engineers. The military lacked experienced commanders. The economy was in ruins, and fear reigned everywhere. Still, Stalin continued to remove all threats to his power. He issued a proclamation that denounced "silent" enemies—those who did not actually commit acts of treason but were guilty because they did not turn in other people.

Up to 2 million executions were carried out, and millions of other people were sent to labor camps in Siberia. In his reign of terror, Stalin even punished the five or six men who were closest to him. In order to keep them loyal, he had their wives and children imprisoned.

By the end of the 1930s, Stalin had created terror solely to bend the country to his will, and he had succeeded. By the end of 1938, he announced a return to "normalcy." The rate of executions slowed considerably, but major political figures were still executed as late as 1940. Stalin's old rival, Trotsky, was murdered in Mexico in August 1940 by an assassin Stalin had sent.

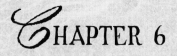

CHAPTER 6

WORLD WAR II AND AFTERMATH

*I*n the 1930s, while Stalin forced his will on the Soviet Union, a similar transformation took place in Western Europe. This was the rise to power of Adolf Hitler and the Nazis in Germany. There were some similarities between Hitler and Stalin. Both had abusive fathers. Both attended religious schools and briefly considered the priesthood. Both had been imprisoned for political activity. Both were outsiders in the nations they ruled—Hitler was from Austria, Stalin from Georgia. Most importantly, both were able to focus public attention on so-called enemies to build their own power. For Stalin, the enemies were the czar, the kulaks, the wreckers, and others. For Hitler, the enemy was the Jews.

Stalin watched the events in Germany carefully, although he had given foreign affairs little attention as his country tried to modernize. Hitler's expansion beyond Germany could not be ignored, however, especially when his powerful Nazi army began to move across Eastern Europe. The Nazis first entered Austria in 1938. Then they occupied the Sudentenland, a German-speaking region of Czechoslovakia in early 1939, and soon took control of the entire nation. The threat of war was a shadow over much of Europe.

Stalin watched the events unfold with a plan in mind. He did not believe that the German army was strong enough to conquer both Western Europe and the Soviet Union. He assumed that if Hitler decided to start an all-out war, the German leader would first send his army west into France and other Western European countries. Stalin felt he could use the Nazis' aggression to his advantage and gain some territory in neighboring Poland. He saw this as a first step toward the spread of the Communist revolution around the world.

To accomplish his goal, yet not alarm the Western powers, Stalin secretly signed a pact with the Germans that agreed to divide Poland between the Soviet Union

Stalin waits to sign the Nonaggression Pact.

and Germany. He planned to wait until Hitler's forces were depleted in Western Europe, then strike across Poland into Germany. Stalin was sure he had beaten Hitler at his own game.

The Nazi-Soviet Nonaggression Pact was signed on August 23, 1939. Stalin gave the Nazis the right to take Lithuania on the Baltic Sea and the western half of Poland, in return for an agreement that the Soviet Union would not be invaded. The Nazis promised the Soviets eastern Poland and eastern Romania, which was located south of Poland. Stalin was delighted with the agreement. It would allow him time to move his entire army halfway across Poland, into position to attack Germany once it weakened.

Stalin did not realize that Hitler was equally devious, and was also eager to sign the Nonaggression Pact. The agreement would free him to take a large amount of Polish territory with minimal resistance. He could then use his armies to conquer Western Europe rather than worry about the Soviet army.

A week after the pact was signed, the Nazis invaded Poland and subdued the western half of the nation within weeks. This invasion, on September 1, 1939, marked the beginning of World War II as England, France, and other nations came to the aid of Poland.

With Poland under their control, Nazi forces concentrated on the Western Front. They invaded France, Belgium, the Netherlands, Norway, and parts of North Africa. Air raids were launched on England. By late 1940, the Nazis almost completely dominated Europe. Hitler then turned back to the Soviet Union.

The Nazi Invasion

Hitler had never intended to honor the Nonaggression Pact with Stalin. He had agreed to it only to keep the

Soviets inactive until his armies controlled the rest of Europe. In June 1941, the Nazis invaded the Soviet Union. By that time, inexperienced Communist Party officers were in charge of the Soviet army. Only one general had survived the purges of the 1930s. The Soviet army collapsed under the onslaught.

Stalin was infuriated. Somehow he had not realized that his purges would lead to this result. For days, he secluded himself in his cottage and refused to meet with any advisers. He believed he was about to lose everything that he had created for himself, and for once, he could only blame himself for his predicament.

What made him angriest was that he had trusted Hitler. Stalin, a man who trusted no one, who had systematically killed off every one of his opponents until he alone reigned supreme, had trusted the leader of a country that had been Russia's bitter enemy in World War I. For once, Stalin had been outwitted by a more diabolical opponent.

After he spent eight days in isolation, a delegation of Communist officials went to see Stalin. They found him seated in a corner of his bedroom. "Why have you come?" he asked, as if he expected to be arrested or removed from power. The men proposed that a Supreme Defense Council be set up, with Stalin at its

German forces destroyed much of the area around Moscow during the invasions.

head, to take control of the war effort. Soon, Stalin had calmed down and set to work just as he had throughout 40 years of violence and revolution. He appealed to the patriotism of his fellow Soviets to fight for their homeland and rout the German invaders. The Soviet people would stand strong and beat back the German barbarians, he declared.

To resist the mighty German war machine was easier said than done. By mid-October, German forces were near Moscow. Soviet troops were poorly trained and their weapons were out-of-date. Early on, Stalin even ordered a cavalry unit into battle against a well-equipped and thoroughly modern German brigade.

83

Fortunately for Stalin, his decision to sign the Nonaggression Pact with Germany was not held against him by Great Britain and the other Allied powers. This alliance now included the United States, which had joined the war against Germany, Japan, and Italy after the Japanese attacked Pearl Harbor, Hawaii, on December 7, 1941. The Allies sent artillery, airplanes, jeeps, armored cars, and other equipment to help the Soviets fight off the German invasion.

Even with modern equipment, the Soviet army was still in disarray. When the Germans reached the outskirts of Moscow in late 1941, the city went into a panic. Families packed their possessions into trucks, carts, and any other vehicles they could find, and fled. Arrangements were made for the government to set up temporary head-quarters in Samara—a city on the banks of the Volga River about 550 miles southeast of Moscow.

Yet Stalin refused to budge. He decided that it would inspire all Soviets if he stayed in Moscow and personally oversaw the coming battle for control of the city. His top army leaders had assured him that the Soviets could win, and he intended to use all his power to make sure it happened.

In the end, it was the harsh Russian winter that saved Moscow from German occupation. By late November

1941, the temperature dropped to -30° F. The wind was so strong and the snow so thick that the soldiers could see only inches in front of them. The Soviets were prepared to handle such conditions. They built shelters, gathered fuel supplies, and wore their warmest winter gear. The Germans, more than 1,000 miles from home, had been so confident of victory when they invaded in June that they had only summer uniforms.

For the remainder of the winter of 1941–1942, Stalin ordered counteroffensives and gained significant ground. Both sides were affected by the weather, and both sides suffered heavy losses. By the spring of 1942, the Nazis and Soviets were in a stalemate.

The Nazi Defeat

While the Nazis waited for warm weather, the Soviets captured a copy of the German attack plan. At first, Stalin refused to believe what his advisers told him was in the plan. It said that the Nazis would not attack Moscow again, but instead would move south to capture territory that was rich in natural resources. The city of Baku was one target because it was a center of the oil industry. The city of Stalingrad, present-day Volgograd, on the Volga River, was another target because it was located on the main waterway that connected the Caspian Sea to Moscow.

The German plan made sense. Yet for all the warning Stalin received, he clung to the belief that the Nazis would attack Moscow. He thought that the intercepted plan was a trick. He thought that Hitler had allowed the document to fall into Soviet hands in order to divert Soviet troops to the south, so that the Germans could take Moscow. With this in mind, Stalin ordered a major offensive.

In May 1942, Soviet forces attacked the Germans, but they were surrounded and defeated. Rather than foil Hitler's plans, Stalin had played right into his hands. Nazi forces now swept toward the Volga River and Caucasus Mountains.

The Battle of Stalingrad, which began in August 1942, may have been the bloodiest battle in history. About 1.3 million Soviet and 800,000 German soldiers lost their lives in a battle that lasted six months. This battle marked a point of no return

Soviet troops charge into battle during the bloody fighting at Stalingrad.

for both sides. Stalin issued an order: "Not one step backwards!" All soldiers who tried to retreat were immediately shot. Hitler, likewise, refused to allow his troops to surrender. He expected his Nazi soldiers to commit suicide rather than be taken alive.

In the early part of August, the German air force bombed major portions of Stalingrad. The purpose was to destroy any means of escape for the Soviets and to make entry for the German ground troops easier. The strategy actually helped the Soviets. The mounds of rubble created throughout the city provided Soviet troops with hideouts and lines of defense. When German armies entered the city, hand-to-hand combat was fought with knives, with pickaxes, and with chunks of rubble and twisted steel.

While the battle raged, the surrounding area was protected by Italian, Romanian, and Hungarian troops—all German allies. As the fight continued in the city through the autumn, however, Stalin ordered a massive buildup of Soviet forces to surround the German allies. When the Soviets attacked from outside the city in late November, the Germans were surrounded by Soviets. Still, Hitler refused to allow his troops to surrender.

The winter of 1942–1943 was every bit as savage as the previous winter. By the middle of January, Soviet forces had cut the German armies in two. Hitler again ordered suicide, but the Germans officially surrendered on February 2, 1943. More than 100,000 Germans were taken prisoner. Fewer than 6,000 would survive. The others would die from cold, disease, starvation, and beatings. The Soviets were able to reclaim much of their own territory and turn the tide against the Nazis. The German armies suffered a disastrous setback from which they never fully recovered.

Victory and Conquest

With the Nazis defeated, Stalin was in the position he had hoped to be in several years earlier. Despite the incredible loss of life, he sent his army across Eastern Europe toward Germany. All the territory that the Soviet army crossed was now part of the rapidly expanding Soviet Union. Stalin's dream of worldwide revolution had been delayed and almost destroyed. By early 1945, however, much of the territory that had been taken by the Nazis in Eastern Europe was in Soviet hands. Control over the people in Poland, Romania, Czechoslovakia, and other countries had passed from Hitler to Stalin.

As it became obvious that the defeat of Germany was inevitable, Allied leaders met to discuss how European territory would be ruled after the war. Stalin met several times with the leader of Great Britain, Winston Churchill, and American president Franklin Roosevelt. In one meeting held in Tehran, Iran, in late 1943, Churchill brought up the subject of what would happen to countries in Eastern Europe after the war. Stalin, whose troops controlled much of that area, said, "there's no need to talk about that. When the time comes we'll have our say." Churchill and Roosevelt left Tehran with the belief that future control of Eastern Europe would be negotiated. In fact, Stalin did not intend to give up control of any of the territory his army held.

On May 7, 1945, the German army surrendered to Allied forces in Berlin, the capital of Germany. Although the Soviet Union was on the victorious side, no country

German generals sign the surrender document in May 1945.

had suffered more: Eight million soldiers and 18 million civilians had been killed in five years of war.

After the bloody war years, it became obvious to many Soviets that Stalin, at 65, had aged considerably. Not only did he look quite a bit older, but he had also slowed mentally and physically. He had always had an excellent memory for names. Now, he could not even recall the names of close associates. He also began to experience bouts of dizziness.

In September 1945, Stalin suffered a minor stroke and spent three months at his vacation cottage on the Black Sea to recuperate. Despite his health problems, Stalin's hold over the Soviet Union remained strong. Most of the territory the Germans had conquered in Eastern Europe had been occupied by Soviet troops on their drive to Berlin at the end of the war. Poland, Finland, Czechoslovakia, Hungary, Bulgaria, Romania, Lithuania, Latvia, Estonia, and even the region of Germany occupied by Soviets during the war, called East Germany, were now under Soviet control. The Bolshevik dream of a Marxist society for the whole world rather than just one nation had come closer to reality.

The influence of Communism also spread into eastern Asia as well. Stalin had declared war on Japan just a week before the war ended. Soviet troops took control

Europe 1945

Areas dominated by the Soviet Union

of territory lost 40 years earlier in the Russo-Japanese War. The Soviet army was then in a position to assist the Communist Chinese in their struggle for control of China. After a violent revolution in the late 1940s,

THE IRON CURTAIN

One of the most admired men of World War II was Winston Churchill, the prime minister of Great Britain. Throughout the darkest days of the Nazi conquest, Churchill's speeches rallied the spirits of people around the world. Shortly before the end of the war, Churchill lost an election and was replaced as prime minister.

Churchill remained very popular in the United States, and in 1946, he went to Westminster College in Fulton, Missouri, to give what became one of the most famous speeches of the twentieth century. Like many people, Churchill was concerned about the spread of communism in the countries that had fallen to Stalin's Soviet forces in the final years of World War II. By 1946, it had become apparent that Stalin intended to keep control over those countries. In his speech, Churchill used what would become a famous phrase to describe the nations of Eastern Europe that seemed to have vanished under Soviet control.

A shadow has fallen upon the scenes so lately lighted by the Allied victory. Nobody knows what Soviet Russia and its Communist international organization intends to do in the immediate future...an iron curtain has descended across the Continent. Behind that line lie all the capitals of the ancient states of Central and Eastern Europe. Warsaw, Berlin, Prague, Vienna, Budapest, Belgrade, Bucharest and Sofia... all...lie in what I must call the Soviet sphere, and all are subject...to Soviet influence...to a very high...measure of control from Moscow....Police governments are prevailing in nearly every case, and...there is no true democracy.

The phrase "iron curtain" instantly became the term used to refer to the countries under Soviet control. The Soviet government was furious. In an interview in *Pravda*, Stalin himself attacked Churchill's views. The phrase, however, continued to be used until the fall of the Soviet Union in 1989.

China installed a Communist government. The Korean Peninsula then became a battleground between Communist and democratic forces, and a civil war broke out.

Stalin and the Soviet Union no longer stood alone against a capitalist world. The influence of the Communist Party was now felt in nations from East Germany to the Pacific Ocean. Yet while Communism and Communist governments arose around the world, Stalin became more worried about threats to his control. During the occupation of Eastern Europe, his troops had seen the wealth of other countries. Stalin remarked often that he feared his troops might be influenced by capitalism they saw. He worried that there would be renewed unrest when the armed forces returned home.

Stalin also began to understand that many Soviets had fought not only for freedom from German conquest, but also for freedom from Soviet oppression. They hoped that the war would usher in a new era for the country without the terror of the 1930s. Yet Stalin knew that without terror, he could not maintain power. With this in mind, he took steps to further tighten his absolute control over the government. In some ways, the terror became even worse.

A flood of new exiles—primarily Soviet soldiers who had been taken as prisoners of war rather than be killed—was sent to labor camps. Others who ended up in prison camps were people who had fought for the Soviet Union, but had remained loyal to their homelands—such as Georgia, Ukraine, and other Soviet-controlled lands. Ethnic groups, such as the Chechens and other minorities, were also sent to Siberia to prevent revolts while the country rebuilt after the war.

The maximum prison camp sentence was increased from 10 to 25 years. A new category of "strict regime" labor camps was developed, where inmates served their time in chains and were not allowed blankets. At the same time, laboratories run by the secret police began to research poisons, mind-altering drugs, and assassination methods, while they implemented new methods of torture for prisoners. The average life span for prisoners was six months.

The Cold War

The renewed terror occurred during a time of international tension between the former allied powers. The world was now dominated by so-called superpowers—the Soviet Union on one side and the United States on the other. There had been indications that this tension would exist since the first meeting between the countries at the end of World War II. In February 1945, a few

94

Winston Churchill, Franklin D. Roosevelt, and Stalin (left to right) met in Yalta to discuss the division of Europe.

months before the end of the war, Stalin met for the second time with Churchill and Roosevelt at Yalta in southern Russia at a palace that had once been a summer retreat of Nicholas II.

At the Yalta Conference, the United States, Soviet Union, and Great Britain agreed that all countries liberated from Nazi control would be allowed to have free elections to decide what kind of government they wanted. As he had done earlier at Tehran, however,

Stalin lied to his allies. By 1946, all the nations of Eastern Europe that had fallen to the Soviet army had Communist governments that reported to Stalin.

Under Stalin's policy, each Eastern European nation's Communist government was loyal to the Soviet Union, and each nation's economy was tied to the economy of the Soviet Union. If Communist control were threatened, each state could use its own army or secret police, or call on the Soviet army and the new secret police, the KGB, for help. The lines between Communist governments and freely elected governments had been drawn.

In February 1946, Stalin gave a speech in which he declared that Communism and capitalism were incompatible. At about the same time, an American diplomat in Moscow, George Kennan, wrote a long memo in which he called Communism the "greatest danger to the free world" and a "parasite which feeds only on diseased tissue."

This exchange of views began the period that became known as the Cold War. The term referred to a conflict between nations that involves high tension but that falls short of all-out war. It was first used by British author George Orwell in 1945. Orwell wrote two novels in the 1940s—*Animal Farm* and *1984*—that criticized states such as the Soviet Union that were under the total control of one person or party.

Truman (center), who took office after Roosevelt's death, met Stalin and Churchill in Potsdam.

The level of tension between the United States and the Soviet Union increased after the development of nuclear weapons. The United States had been the first to make and use an atomic bomb. At a meeting in Potsdam, Netherlands, in 1945, President Harry S. Truman, who had taken office after Roosevelt's death, told Stalin that the United States had developed a new secret weapon. Truman had imagined that news of this superweapon would shock Stalin. Stalin, however, was not surprised. Soviet spies had kept him informed of the development of the atomic bomb, and he had Soviet scientists at work on such a weapon, too.

The first Soviet atomic bomb was successfully exploded in a test in August 1949. At that point, the two most powerful nations in the world had weapons of mass destruction. By 1950, the Cold War was the main focus of U.S. and Soviet foreign policy. The two countries never actually went to war. To fight each other, they gave support to the enemies of the other side in Asia and Africa.

The Painful Death

By 1951, Soviet scientists had created atomic bombs that were more than twice as powerful as those the United States had dropped on Japan to end World War II. The bombs were also much lighter than American bombs. Stalin began to urge his scientists to develop missiles that could carry the atomic weapons thousands of miles to a target.

As he entered his final years, Stalin planned to end the Cold War in a "Great War with the West." This war, he believed, would finally destroy capitalism. He was prepared to build a worldwide Marxist society through the use of nuclear weapons.

While his scientists worked to create bombs and missiles, Stalin turned his fury on those he now believed were a threat in the country—the people he called the "agents of capitalism"—the Jews. A wave of anti-Semitism spread throughout the Soviet Union, and many Jews were imprisoned.

As large as Stalin's dreams were, his health did not allow him to reach his goal. He had become an increasingly heavy drinker, and his heart had weakened since his stroke several years earlier. In the spring of 1952, his doctor advised him to take a rest from politics for health reasons. Stalin remembered that this was exactly what had happened to Lenin as he was eased from the political scene so that others could take over. In fact, Stalin himself had been in charge of that takeover. He immediately ordered the arrest and torture of all the leading Kremlin doctors, as well as certain military doctors.

In 1953, the doctors were supposed to have been publicly tried and then hanged in the middle of Red Square. In addition, plans were already under way to remove all Soviet Jews from the rest of society and resettle them in a far eastern territory of the country. March 5, 1953, was the day the resettlement was to begin. A different event prevented the resettlement.

Stalin was always a late riser, who routinely stayed up and drank until 4 or 5 o'clock in the morning and then slept until noon or early afternoon. On March 1, 1953, his bodyguard heard movement inside Stalin's quarters around midday. Although the guard became uneasy when Stalin did not make an appearance during the afternoon, he did not become alarmed until evening.

Lights in the house were turned on at 6:30 P.M., but Stalin still did not emerge. At 10:30 that night, officials broke down the door and entered the living quarters. A deputy secretary found Stalin on the carpet by a table. He had not lost consciousness, but he was unable to speak. He was carried to a couch. Senior officials were called, and they arrived at various times throughout the night. Stalin seemed to sleep comfortably. No doctors were called until the next morning.

When the doctors arrived, they discovered that a blood vessel in Stalin's brain had burst. For the next three days, he received treatment—various injections and medications—and was even treated with leeches to try to relieve the hemorrhage in his brain. At times, he seemed to rally, but overall, he grew steadily worse.

The memoirs of Stalin's daughter, Svetlana, describe his final hours on March 5, 1953:

> *For the last twelve hours, the lack of oxygen became acute. His face and lips blackened as he suffered slow strangulation. The death agony was terrible. He literally choked to death as we watched. At what seemed like the very last moment, he opened his eyes and cast a glance over everyone in the room. It was a terrible glance, insane or perhaps angry, and full*

After his death, Stalin lay in state for Soviet citizens to pay their respects.

of fear of death. . . . He suddenly lifted his left hand as though he were pointing to something up above and bringing down a curse on all. The gesture was incomprehensible and full of menace. . . . He died a difficult and terrible death.

Stalin said that "a single death is a tragedy," but for the people of the Soviet Union, and perhaps for the entire world, his own death was fortunate. Had he lived, millions more people—those Stalin called "statistics"— might have died. In the end, one of the greatest villains of history, who caused unimaginable agony to millions, died slowly and painfully.

CHRONOLOGY

1879   Stalin is born.

1894   Stalin enters Tiflis Theological Seminary.

1898   First Congress of the Russian Social Democratic Party.

1903   Social Democratic Party splits into Mensheviks and Bolsheviks.

1905   Stalin meets Vladimir Lenin.

Revolution of 1905 and first Russian constitution.

1912   Stalin named by Lenin to Bolshevik Party Central Committee.

1917   Bolsheviks force Nicholas II from throne; Russia withdraws from World War I.

1918–1921   Civil war results from Bolshevik attempts to collectivize industry and agriculture.

1922   Lenin appoints Stalin general secretary of the Communist Party.

1924   Lenin dies.

1929   Stalin introduces five-year plans to bring the Soviet Union into the modern industrial age.

Stalin becomes dictator of the Soviet Union after outwitting his rivals.

1932–33	Seven million people die in famine in Ukraine.
1935	Great purge of Communist Party membership begins.
1937	Stalin begins a purge of Red army generals.
1939	Soviet Union signs the Nazi-Soviet Nonaggression Pact with Germany.
1941	Germany invades Soviet Union
1942	Battle of Stalingrad begins.
1943	Germans surrender at Stalingrad in the first major defeat of Hitler's armies.
1945	Soviet troops reach Berlin, Germany.
1946	Soviet forces retain control of Eastern Europe after World War II; Cold War begins
1949	Soviet Union explodes atomic bomb.
1953	Stalin dies in Moscow on March 5.

Glossary

Allies The nations that fought against Germany, Italy, and Japan in World War II: Great Britain, France, the Soviet Union, and the United States (among others).

Bolsheviks Members of the Russian Social Democratic Party who believed in the violent overthrow of the czarist government.

communism A political system in which there is no private property.

collectivization A system of government control over industrial and agricultural production.

czar Ruler of Russia before the revolution.

exile To send away from one's country or home.

famine An extreme shortage of food.

Marxism A political system in which workers rule a classless society.

Mensheviks Members of the Russian Social Democratic Party who believed in the gradual transition to a Marxist government.

propaganda Information spread to influence or mislead people.

socialism A system of governmental ownership of goods.

Source Notes

Introduction
Page 5: "devil's hoof." Radzinsky, Edward. *Stalin*. New York: Anchor Books, 1996 p. 29.

Chapter 1
Page 11: "bitter rude . . . child." Radzinsky, p. 25.

Page 14 : "A nation of slaves." Ibid p. 33.

Page 16: "unite with the savage world . . . " Ibid p. 35.

Page 20: "I joined the revolutionary movement . . ." Ibid p 36.

Chapter 2
Page 26: "Ally yourself with the criminal world." Ibid p. 35.

Page 27: "Koba passed between the ranks . . ." Ibid p. 50.

Page 33: "the murder of policemen . . ." Ibid p. 57.

Page 37: "She softened my heart . . ." Ibid p. 65.

Chapter 3
Page 40: "I've got no provisions . . ." Ibid p 77.

Page 49: "Our hand will not tremble . . ." Ibid p. 148.

Chapter 4
Page 56: "Stalin, having become . . ." Website *Lenin Internet Archive* http://www.marxists.org/archive/lenin/works/1922/dec/testamnt/congress.htm

Chapter 5
Page 64: "If one person dies . . ." Website *Brainy quotes* http://www.brainyquote.com/quotes/quotes/j/q128088.html

Page 70: "Conditions in the Ukraine . . ." Website *The Ukrainian Weekly* http://www.ukrweekly.com/Archive/Great_Famine/

Page 72: "A comrade dear to us" Radzinsky p. 288.

Page 76: "The New Czar" Ibid p. 24.

Chapter 6
Page 82: "Why have you come?" Radzinsky p. 470.

Page 87: "Not one step backwards!" Ibid p. 488.

Page 89: "There's no need to talk about that . . ." Ibid p. 497.

Page 92: "A shadow has fallen..." Website *Modern History Sourcebook*
http://www.fordham.edu/halsall/mod/churchill-iron.html

Page 96: "the greatest danger..." Website *The History Guide*
http://www.historyguide.org/europe/kennan.html

Page 100: "For the last twelve hours..." Radzinsky p. 576.

For Further Reading

Downing, David. *Joseph Stalin* (Leading Lives). Portsmouth, NH: Heinemann, 2001.

Kallen, Stuart A. *Before the Communist Revolution: Russian History Before 1919*. New York: ABDO & Daughters, 1992.

Matthews, John R. *The Rise and Fall of the Soviet Union*. San Diego: Lucent Books, 2000.

Willoughby, Susan. *The Russian Revolution*. Portsmouth, NH: Heinemann, 1996.

Wood, Alan. *Stalin and Stalinism*. London: Routledge, 1990.

Websites

The Path to Revolution
http://www.geographia.com/russia/rushis06.htm
Good overview of the Bolshevik rise to power.

Stalin
http://www.dickinson.edu/~history/dictators/Stalin.htm
Excellent biography with details of life in the Soviet
  Union during the Stalin era.

Joseph Stalin
http://gi.grolier.com/wwii/wwii_stalin.html
Concise biography with some interesting detail about
  Stalin's personality.

Stalin, Joseph
http://www.encyclopedia.com/html/S/Stalin-J.asp
Good biography divided into four phases, includes a
  bibliography.

Index